Original title:
The Laughing Log

Copyright © 2025 Creative Arts Management OÜ
All rights reserved.

Author: Alec Donovan
ISBN HARDBACK: 978-1-80567-249-4
ISBN PAPERBACK: 978-1-80567-548-8

Resonance of the Playful Pines

In a glade where whispers dance,
The tallest trees wear silly pants.
Branches sway in jovial glee,
A call for laughter, wild and free.

Dancing shadows skip and twirl,
As squirrels in acorns spin and whirl.
With every breeze, a chuckle floats,
Tickling leaves on joyful coats.

Beneath the bark, a secret joke,
The woodpecker's tap, a merry poke.
Nature's jest, so light and bright,
Turning day into pure delight.

Gather round, ye merry folk,
Hear the calls, and take a stroke.
With every giggle, laughter binds,
In the forest's heart, joy unwinds.

Amusement Among the Oaks

In the shade where whispers dance,
Squirrels prance and birds take chance.
Laughter spills from every tree,
While deer giggle with wild glee.

Breezes tickle leaves so green,
A merry sight, a joyful scene.
Frogs croak jokes by the stream,
Nature's laughter, a sweet dream.

The Forest of Frolics

In the woods where shadows play,
Mischief hides in light of day.
Bunnies bounce with little hops,
Chasing tails and funny flops.

Whispers of the wind engage,
Every creature on the stage.
Chirping crickets join the fun,
When the setting sun is done.

Jolly Jingles of the Wild

Rustling leaves in merry glow,
Echoes of a lively show.
Raccoons spin in leaps and bounds,
Chasing giggles all around.

A chorus of the carefree throng,
Nature's choir sings along.
Even the wise old owl will joke,
As laughter rises like a smoke.

Giggles from the Ground

Underneath the sunny skies,
Little ants share silly sighs.
Grass blades bend to hear the cheer,
As critters draw their friends near.

The muddy piglet takes a slip,
Sending splashes with each flip.
Frolicsome spirits fill the air,
With chuckles floating everywhere.

Happy Saplings

In the grove where giggles sway,
Tiny trees dance in playful display.
Leaves flutter like hats on the breeze,
Branches waving with mischievous tease.

Squirrels play tag on trunks so stout,
While sparrows bob and twist about.
Roots tap their toes, a rhythmic delight,
Nature's jovial party, pure and bright.

Breezy Chuckles

Whispers float on the zephyr's song,
With every chuckle, we can't go wrong.
Mossy rocks wear smiles so wide,
As sunlight beams, we laugh and glide.

Frogs croak jokes from their lily pads,
While rabbits nudge with cheeky jabs.
The brook joins in with a giddy splash,
Creating a symphony of joyous bash.

Woodland Whimsy

In the glade where shadows play,
Mushrooms twirl, inviting the fray.
Fireflies giggle, blinking bright,
As the moon dons a glow, playful and light.

Chipmunks wear tiny little masks,
As they scamper through their fun-filled tasks.
The forest whispers secrets, a mirthful dance,
Inviting all within its funny expanse.

Sprightly Spirits of the Forest

Elves in the branches, with laughter so free,
Spin tales of mischief 'neath the old apple tree.
Breezes carry chuckles, a playful delight,
While shadows hop and frolic in the night.

The laughter echoing through bushes and glen,
Calls out to all, come join in again.
For every twig has a story to tell,
In this merry realm where whimsy dwells.

Chasing Shadows of Joy

In a forest bright and free,
Shadows dance with glee,
They play tag with the trees,
Hiding behind bark with ease.

Giggles echo through the air,
As whispers float without a care,
Each leaf shimmers, laughs unwind,
In every nook, joy is entwined.

Revelry in Rings

Circles of laughter, round and wide,
Entwined like friends, side by side,
Giggling rings upon the ground,
Where silly secrets abound.

With every twist, a chuckle blooms,
In playful spirals, joy consumes,
Nature's dance, a merry song,
Inviting all to join along.

Mirthful Moments in the Meadow

In a meadow full of cheer,
Butterflies twirl, no hint of fear,
Daffodils sway, laughing bright,
As sunshine bathes in golden light.

A rabbit hops, a jest well played,
While shadows stretch in playful shade,
Each blink of grass brings joy anew,
With laughing skies of endless blue.

Tickled Bark

Funny faces carved with cheer,
Upon the trunks, they draw near,
Giggling rings of bark create,
A wooden world, oh what a fate!

Whispers tickle, laughter grows,
As creatures peek from their cozy throes,
Woodland whimsies, sweet and bright,
Launching joy into the night.

Frothy murmurs of Nature's Heart

In the glade where whispers play,
A brook giggles through the day.
Mossy stones join in the fun,
Chasing shadows, away they run.

Butterflies dance, a silly sight,
Tickled petals, sheer delight.
Every rustle, a chuckling sound,
Nature's laughter all around.

Revelry in the Roots and Rings

Beneath the boughs, a raucous cheer,
Squirrels chime in, all appear.
With acorn hats and leafy capes,
They spin around in joyful scrapes.

The wise old tree with knots so grand,
Chortles softly, takes a stand.
As twigs throw jokes, and branches sway,
Life's parade, come join the fray.

Playful Spirits of the Woodlands

Within the thicket, laughter lies,
Glimmering winks, and teasing sighs.
Mischievous winds tickle the leaves,
Delighting every soul who believes.

The fireflies wink, mischief bright,
Adventurous souls with hearts alight.
Their laughter echoes, a playful tune,
Under the mischievous moon.

Mirth of the Moss-Covered Giant

A giant rests in emerald dress,
With cheeks so round, he loves to jest.
He shakes with glee, his branches sway,
As critters gather, ready to play.

Sunbeams slip through, casting rays,
Illuminating his colorful ways.
With every chuckle, the forest beams,
Joy weaves through their sunlight dreams.

Whispers of Woodland Whimsy

In the woods where shadows dance,
Squirrels chatter, laughing a chance.
Mushrooms pop like tiny caps,
As the breeze plays silly taps.

Frogs wear hats of green and gold,
Telling tales, both strange and bold.
With every gust, the branches sway,
Creating jokes in a playful way.

Giggling Boughs Beneath the Sky

Beneath the sky, the branches giggle,
As acorns bounce and birds begin to wiggle.
Laughter floats on the warm sunlight,
With every rustle, everything feels bright.

The flowers bloom with cheeky grins,
Tickling bees as the fun begins.
A playful breeze, a soft little tease,
Makes the whole glade feel at ease.

Echoes in the Enchanted Grove

In the grove where laughter sings,
The daisies twirl on unseen strings.
A rabbit hops, and suddenly trips,
Spilling joy from its little lips.

Echoes ring from tree to tree,
Rustling leaves join in with glee.
Nature chuckles, a merry sound,
Where silly moments can be found.

Chuckles of the Ancient Tree

An ancient tree with twisted bark,
Cracks a smile; oh, what a lark!
Its branches sway with a hearty laugh,
Creating shadows, a quirky path.

Beneath its shade, the critters play,
Chasing giggles through the day.
With every stir, a chuckle grows,
In this haven where joy overflows.

Sprightly Spirits in the Shade

Beneath the boughs where shadows play,
Frolicsome whispers chase the day.
Squirrels dance in merry flight,
While sunlight giggles, warm and bright.

Jolly breezes softly tease,
Rustling leaves like joyous pleas.
A fountain of chuckles flits around,
As nature's wonders spin profound.

A trickster frog leaps to the beat,
Splashing laughter at our feet.
Joyful chirps in harmony sing,
In this realm where cheekiness is king.

With every rustle, a surprise found,
In leafy crowns where joy abounds.
Sprightly spirits will never fade,
In this green world of jokes well-made.

Glee in Nature's Embrace

In the meadow, smiles take flight,
Bouncing daisies, pure delight.
Butterflies wear gowns of cheer,
Gliding softly, drawing near.

Giggles of streams twist and twine,
Reflecting sparkles, oh so fine.
Laughter echoes, sweet and clear,
Nature's chorus draws us near.

Jumping worms in dirt disguise,
Leaping plants with jovial sighs.
The sun winks through leaves that sway,
A playful scene in bright display.

Each nook and cranny, joy's own space,
With blooms that dance in warm embrace.
In nature's glee, our spirits blaze,
In this whimsied, gleeful maze.

Nature's Joyous Blooms

Petals burst in colors bold,
Whispering secrets, tales untold.
Bees with laughter buzz and hum,
In every bloom, a happy drum.

Tulips nod with cheeky grace,
While daisies grin in sunny place.
The garden's secret, bright and clear,
Joyful nature's laughter here.

In the breeze, the flowers sway,
Telling jokes the clouds display.
Vivid hues and scents combine,
In this lively, laughing design.

From dawn till dusk, the blossoms cheer,
Spreading joy, their charms sincere.
In this patch of vibrant hues,
Nature's giggles, we can't refuse.

Forest of the Jolly Echoes

Among the trees, a laughter lingers,
Whistling winds tease playful fingers.
Chirping notes in harmony rise,
As woodland critters jest and surprise.

Mushrooms giggle in their spots,
Each a ghost of laughter's thoughts.
Swaying branches, such a sight,
Tickle our hearts with pure delight.

A wise old owl, with twinkling eye,
Keeps a secret, a merry why.
With every rustle, every cheer,
He spins a tale for those who hear.

In colors lush and shadows deep,
The forest sings us all to sleep.
Where laughter blooms like flowers bright,
In every echo, joy takes flight.

Merry Resonance

In the wood where echoes play,
A squirrel dances, hip-hip-hooray!
Leaves whisper tales of chuckling trees,
Nature's laughter floats on the breeze.

Bouncing beetles, such comedic sprites,
Caterpillars in twirling tights.
Every branch holds a giggling tune,
A sunbeam winks, the day's a boon.

Uproar in the Underbrush

A hedgehog spins, a curious sight,
While a rabbit hops with sheer delight.
The grasshoppers chirp a merry score,
As frogs join in with a ribbit roar.

Beneath the ferns, a party brews,
With all the critters sporting shoes.
Bursts of laughter, a joyful shout,
In the underbrush, no room for doubt.

Nectar of Joy

Honeybees buzz with jokes to share,
While ladybugs laugh without a care.
Sweet nectar spills from blooms above,
A sweetened gift, like laughter's love.

Each cheeky ant tells tales of glee,
As butterflies flaunt their jubilee.
Petals dance in a hilarious swirl,
This garden's laced with joy, oh world!

Grinning in the Green

In fields so lush, the daisies grin,
As cheery critters twirl and spin.
Witty words from a playful breeze,
Tickling the toes of buzzing bees.

The sunbeams tease, a radiant beam,
While shadows play a comical dream.
With every rustle, a new delight,
In the green we laugh from morning till night.

Woodland Merrymaking

In the glade where shadows play,
Squirrels dance in bright array.
Frogs croak tunes to trees so tall,
Nature's laughter echoes, a joyous call.

With acorns flying in a spree,
Rabbits hop with glee, oh, see!
A turtle chuckles, slow and wise,
While fireflies blink like little spies.

Gleeful Growth

Mushrooms wiggle, head held high,
Tickled by breezes that flutter by.
Roots entwine in a comical jig,
As flowers swirl, in bloom, they dig.

Butterflies burst forth in flight,
Spreading joy with colors bright.
A caterpillar grins, so pleased,
Wiggling through greens, the forest teased.

Laughing Leaves

Leaves quiver and giggle in the sun,
Waiting for breezes, oh what fun!
Swaying with mirth in endless rows,
Telling sweet tales that everyone knows.

A woodpecker knocks to join the cheer,
Jokes shared with each chirp, oh so near.
Rustling whispers through branches lean,
Bringing smiles to the forest scene.

A Giggle Beneath Branches

Beneath the trees, where shadows twist,
Squirrels chuckle, too hard to resist.
A raccoon twirls in whimsical spin,
While the sun peeks through with a cheeky grin.

Old trunks contain secrets quite rare,
Stories of laughter float in the air.
As day wanes, the fun won't cease,
Nature's humor, a never-ending feast.

Woodland Giggles Beneath the Stars

In the quiet glade, where shadows dance,
A squirrel mocks, in silly prance.
Owls chuckle softly, under moon's glow,
As fireflies wink, putting on a show.

The wise old tree hums a tune of glee,
With branches swaying, a whimsical spree.
Crickets provide the rhythm, so bold,
As night wraps laughter in stories untold.

Rustic Humor in the Sunlight

Beneath the sun's warm embrace,
A rabbit plays an amusing race.
Twirling leaves, a playful tease,
While the brook giggles with the breeze.

Mice share jokes with acorns near,
Their laughter spreading, crystal clear.
Nature crafts this merry scene,
Where joy can sprout in shades of green.

Banter in the Bark

Beneath the bark, tales intertwine,
As beetles argue, claiming a line.
A witty woodpecker taps and dives,
Sharing punchlines that come alive.

In every notch, humor resides,
Where whispers of laughter happily hides.
Foxes chirp with fox-like flair,
While all around, giggles fill the air.

Woodland Riddles of Delight

Amidst the ferns, riddles abound,
With every glance, joy can be found.
A dandelion winks, as if to say,
Life is a game; come join the play!

The sun spills laughter on every leaf,
Weaving mirth into scenes beyond belief.
Bunny secrets and tales of sass,
In this playful glen, time will not pass.

Giggles in the Glade

In the woods where shadows play,
Squirrels dance throughout the day.
They twirl and leap in sunny rays,
Joyful antics on display.

With every rustle, every cheer,
The forest hums, it's crystal clear.
Whispers of laughter ring so near,
Nature's jesters, never drear.

The flowers giggle, petals bright,
Wiggling roots in pure delight.
Beneath the branches, quite a sight,
A symphony of pure excite.

So come and play, leave cares behind,
In this glade, pure joy you'll find.
With every chuckle, hearts entwined,
Nature's magic, sweetly kind.

Mirthful Bark

On gnarled limbs where laughter's sewn,
Whimsical creatures make their home.
From tree to tree, they love to roam,
In funny hats, they find their zone.

Beneath the boughs, the jesters meet,
Sharing tales of mischief sweet.
Acorns tumble at their feet,
While giggles burst, a rhythmic beat.

The old oak shakes in hearty glee,
As riddles float on breezy spree.
Branches sway, a dance to see,
In every laugh, they feel so free.

So hear the joy, let spirits spark,
In this playful realm, ignite the spark.
Every leaf, a chuckle, hark!
Come join the fun, embrace the lark!

Chortles Beneath the Canopy

Underneath the leafy dome,
Chortles rise like clouds of foam.
Witty banter finds its home,
In every nook, a friendly poem.

The bashful bunnies in a race,
With wiggles, hops, and funny face.
The sunbeams play a shining chase,
Unraveling giggles, sweet embrace.

With every breeze, a tickling tease,
The trees sway low, their limbs at ease.
From silly sounds, they aim to please,
A mirthful world that will not freeze.

So gather round, and don't be shy,
Let laughter blend with the sky.
In whispers soft, you'll hear them sigh,
In jubilation, spirits fly.

Laughter in Timber

Softly giggles swirl around,
Echoes of joy in nature found.
Woodland friends with hearts unbound,
In playful antics, life abounds.

Up in the boughs, the robins sing,
While chipmunks scamper, joy they bring.
The mossy banks with laughter cling,
As laughter ripples, blossoming.

With every rustle, laughter reigns,
Even the streams wear silly chains.
Nature's smiles are swapped like gains,
A tapestry of joyful plains.

So let us roam where chuckles thrive,
In timbered halls, feel joy alive.
With every grin, our hearts contrive,
A world so funny, we will dive.

Chuckles by the Stream

Bubbles rise and giggles float,
Where smooth stones become a boat.
Frogs in hats, they croak with glee,
Dancing jigs beside the tree.

The water tickles toes so bare,
Splashing friends with merry air.
A turtle grins, his shell a laugh,
As minnows chase a wiggling path.

Squirrels swing from branch to branch,
Playing peek-a-boo; what a chance!
Their chatter blends with nature's song,
In this realm where joy belongs.

Laughter bubbles in the sun,
Every moment bright and fun.
Nature's stage, a comedy,
Where smiles bloom like flowers free.

Glee in the Grove

A funny hat on a chipmunk's head,
With tiny shoes, history's wed.
Dancing mushrooms sway in cheer,
While giggling breezes whisper near.

Twisting vines do the tango bold,
Underneath a sun so gold.
A parrot cracks a joke, quite loud,
While clouds gather, heaven's crowd.

The breeze plays tricks, it pulls your hair,
A chorus of chuckles fills the air.
Bouncing berries, they roll with zest,
In this merry grove, all feel blessed.

Every leaf shares a secret grin,
For laughter's echo draws you in.
In every nook, there's light to gleam,
This is a place where dreams redeem.

Playful Shadows

In the twilight, shadows leap,
Tickling toes, they gently creep.
Whispers float, like tales of old,
They spin each yarn with laughter bold.

Dancing lights that twinkle bright,
Chasing stars, a comical sight.
The moon joins in, a silver smile,
As night unfolds its playful style.

Bumbling bugs, with clumsy flight,
Gather round for fun each night.
With every crash, a hearty cheer,
Echoes of joy for all to hear.

Each flicker brings a jest anew,
A symphony of giggles, too.
In shadows' play, we find our bliss,
For in the dark, we can't resist.

Jests of the Forest

Among the trees, a riddle spun,
Where oak and pine share jokes in fun.
A hedgehog winks, a secret shared,
With every chuckle, none is spared.

Woodpeckers drum, a lively beat,
As nature's band presents its feat.
The wind's a jester, full of tricks,
Whirling leaves like cartwheel flicks.

Rabbits in bow ties leap, they say,
"Join our circus, come and play!"
With laughter loud, they prance around,
In this green world, joy is found.

Each branch a stage, each nook a jest,
In this forest, we are blessed.
So let us cheer, and bond with cheer,
For jests and laughter bring us near.

The Giggling Grove

In the shade where whispers play,
Leaves chuckle in a breezy ballet.
Squirrels dance on branches high,
While butterflies waltz in the sky.

The flowers snicker, colors grand,
Tickled by a gentle hand.
Bunnies hop with comic flair,
Every golden beam a dare.

Rabbits roll on soft green beds,
Jokers wear enchanted threads.
In this place of joyful cheer,
Laughter blooms from ear to ear.

Winds will sing a playful tune,
Underneath the beaming moon.
In this grove of glee and jest,
Nature hosts a humor fest.

Happy Hues of Nature

In a rainbow of glowing glades,
Sun-kissed hills wear laughter's shades.
Joyful whispers twist and twirl,
Nature's joy, a bright-eyed whirl.

Daisies smile where shadows blend,
Frogs in ponds with voices send.
Sunflowers nod with witty grace,
Each petal holds a funny face.

Breezes tease with playful sighs,
Clouds drift by in goofy ties.
Colors prance in vibrant scenes,
Nature's palette bursts at the seams.

In every nook, good times arise,
Amid the laughter that complies.
Happy hues twinkle bright and clear,
Where every moment brings a cheer.

Sprightly Shapes

Mushrooms dance in patterned fleet,
While chubby toads skip on their feet.
Hearts of pine trees sway and sway,
Tickling each breeze that comes their way.

Wooly clouds yawn in sunshine's reign,
Unruly giggles, light as rain.
Breezy shapes parade along,
To a nature's silly song.

Blossoms burst in joyful fray,
As playful breezes make them sway.
Caterpillars twirl with glee,
In their silken jubilee.

Nature's canvas, bright and keen,
Crafts a scene, so lightly seen.
Sprightly shapes in every nook,
Invite you in with every look.

Nature's Buoyant Breath

Puffing clouds in fluffy glee,
Blow soft wishes that soar free.
Giggles bubble from the brook,
As nature shares her merry hook.

Merriment dances on each leaf,
Winking stars bring comic relief.
Rosy dusk with jesters bright,
Colors swirl in endless flight.

Crickets chirp with cheeky chats,
While wise old owls spin their hats.
Sunrise quips in golden rays,
Launching joy into the days.

Nature's breath, a vibrant cheer,
Filling hearts with laughter near.
In every moment, joy, we find,
In nature's arms, we're all entwined.

Fables of the Frolicsome

In the grove where shadows play,
A squirrel pops and twirls away,
With acorns tossed in silly dance,
Each fluttering leaf joins in, perchance.

The wise old owl, with eyes so wide,
Chuckles softly as he hides,
While rabbits tumble, roll, and spin,
In this joyful race, no one can win.

A river sings with gurgles loud,
Echoes of fun gather a crowd,
In every splash, a tale unfolds,
Of frolicsome hearts, forever bold.

With twilight charm, stars wink and glow,
As crickets chirp their nightly show,
The forest buzzes with hearty cheer,
In fables spun, the world draws near.

Woodland Laughter

Amidst the trees where sunlight beams,
A raccoon shares his wildest dreams,
His tales of cheese and midnight feasts,
Bring smiles alive, to say the least.

The fox trots in, with a crafty grin,
Telling of mischief, where to begin,
Each pawprint leads to riotous fun,
Underneath the warm golden sun.

A bouncy hare hops high with glee,
Counting stars one, two, and three,
In whimsical bounds amidst the glen,
Where laughter echoes, time and again.

As dusk enfolds in hues so bright,
The woods are alive—what a delightful sight,
With joyous hearts and giggles in the air,
The merry woodland holds secrets rare.

Cheerful Whispers in the Wind

In breezy whispers, tales are spun,
The tale of a chipmunk who loves to run,
He zips through flowers like a sprightly breeze,
Tickling petals, planting teasing tease.

The butterflies giggle, dance through the air,
Winking at bees without a care,
They play tag on the warm summer loom,
While sunbeams beam, dispelling gloom.

A wise old turtle, slow but sly,
Shares secret jokes before the sky,
His laughter bubbles in ripples shy,
Like giggling streams that flutter by.

As day transforms to night so sweet,
Stars sprinkle laughter on those they meet,
Each twinkle holds a giggling tune,
In joyful fields beneath the moon.

The Playful Canopy

Underneath branches where shadows prance,
The bumblebee sways in a funny dance,
Spinning circles 'round flowers bright,
While ants march on, in pure delight.

A parrot laughs with a beak so wide,
Mimicking giggles from every side,
His rainbow feathers flutter and sway,
As whispers of joy, in a playful way.

The merry raccoon, with his mask held tight,
Juggles pine cones in the glow of twilight,
With each dropped nut, a chuckle goes,
In this enchanting place, laughter grows.

As twilight weaves a dreamlike skein,
Creatures waltz in a joyous refrain,
With nature's heart, they weave and spin,
In playful shimmers, where fun begins.

Nature's Joyful Chorus

In the meadow, giggles spring,
As the daisies start to sing.
Breezes carry silly sounds,
Laughter dances all around.

Squirrels play tag with the breeze,
In the trees, they swing with ease.
Butterflies flit to and fro,
Painting joy wherever they go.

Underneath the sunny trees,
Songs of joy, as light as peas.
Nature's fun is on display,
In this light, we laugh and play.

Bubbles rise from rivers bright,
Winking at the new daylight.
Every creature, big and small,
Joining in the merry call.

Sunlit Giggles

When sunlight spills on grassy green,
Tickled leaves are seen between.
Petals blush with sunny cheer,
Whispers of joy for all who hear.

Bouncing bunnies with a hop,
Skips and jumps, they never stop.
Sunbeams twirl, they join the fun,
Chasing shadows, everyone.

Clouds puff up, a cotton dream,
With every laugh, the flashes beam.
Nature's theater, bright and bold,
Playful tales are there to unfold.

Silly birds with colors bright,
Chirping songs from morn till night.
In this world of vibrant glee,
Every laugh feels wild and free.

Radiance of Raucousness

At sunrise, giggles rise anew,
Radiant beams of golden hue.
The flowers sway in raucous song,
In this space, we all belong.

Around the brook, frogs jive and dive,
Splashing joy, they feel alive.
Dancing ants in a wiggly line,
Nature's fun, so sweet and fine.

Windy whispers tickle the trees,
Frolicsome tales float with the breeze.
Every branch tells tales of cheer,
Chortles echo everywhere here.

Puffy clouds with silly shapes,
Bring to mind the joyful tapes.
In this laughter, life's delight,
Every day feels fresh and bright.

Frivolous Foliage

Green leaves laugh with a twist and shout,
In the forest, there's no doubt.
Every branch plays peek-a-boo,
Jokes and jests for me and you.

Lush vines dance in playful fun,
Chasing shadows on the run.
Dancing leaves under the sun,
Frivolous moments, everyone.

Forest critters share a joke,
Making mischief by the oak.
With each chuckle, spirits soar,
Nature's whimsy we adore.

Laughing flowers seem to wink,
Inviting us to pause and think.
In this garden of delight,
Every heart feels warm and bright.

Nature's Chuckling Canvas

In fields where flowers dance and play,
The wind is giggling all the way.
A butterfly with a silly face,
Flits about like it owns the place.

Bumblebees buzz with a comical hum,
While ants march in a jolly strum.
Trees sway, shake a leafy grin,
Nature laughs where silly begins.

Blissful Burrows

In the earth where rabbits dwell,
Their tiny homes are stories to tell.
With wiggles and hops, they play hide and seek,
In a world where giggles are far from meek.

Mice in a maze, a comedic chase,
Scurrying about with such a pace.
Their tiny squeaks like laughter resound,
In cozy burrows, joy can be found.

Trees That Tell Tales

Beneath the branches, secrets are spun,
Of squirrels who joke in the warm sun.
Knots in the bark wear expressions wide,
  Whispers of laughter in every stride.

A raccoon at dusk, with a mischief spark,
Dances with shadows, not afraid of the dark.
Each tree a witness to giggles and glee,
  Nature's own comedy, wild and free.

Joy in the Wilderness

Amidst the wild where the critters prance,
Life unfolds like a joyful dance.
With each rustling leaf, there's a cheerful sound,
A symphony of chuckles all around.

The brook bubbles up with a playful trick,
Rocks giggle softly, never too slick.
In this vibrant world, happiness flows,
Wilderness laughter that endlessly grows.

Timber Tales of Timeless Glee

In the woods where shadows play,
Trees tell tales of bright array.
Squirrels giggle, dance so free,
Beneath the branches, joy we see.

Rabbits hop with bouncy cheer,
Whispers echo, laughter near.
Roots and vines, a playful crew,
Nature's jest, a funny view.

Mice with hats spin round and round,
Chasing each other on the ground.
Logs that roll and laugh so loud,
Bring a smile to every crowd.

Breezes blow with teasing jest,
Every creature feels so blessed.
Timber tales, both wild and grand,
In this forest, joy we stand.

Whimsy in the Wilds

On a branch, a bird does perch,
Singing songs, a funny search.
With a wink and a merry cheer,
Nature's humor brought us here.

Bunny tails and floppy ears,
Dance around, it seems so clear.
With a hop, they tease the breeze,
Tickling grass beneath the trees.

Frogs in coats jump to the beat,
Croaking jests, their froggy feat.
Laughter bubbles in the stream,
In this world, we share a dream.

Sunlight filters, twinkling bright,
Leaves are chuckling, what delight!
In the wild, where joy's in sight,
Every moment feels so right.

Joyful Leaves in a Breezy Dance

Leaves are twirling, having fun,
Waving 'hello' to everyone.
With a flutter, they make a jest,
In this breeze, we feel so blessed.

Branches sway, a playful show,
Whispers soft, as breezes blow.
Tall trees chuckle, roots hold tight,
In this dance, all feels just right.

Acorns tumble, roll along,
Nature hums a silly song.
With each step, the forest prances,
In the joy, the spirit dances.

Sun-kissed glades of green delight,
Bringing laughter, pure and bright.
In this stage, where all can play,
Fun and folly rule the day.

Chortles from the Verdant Abyss

In the depths where shadows roam,
Laughter echoes, feels like home.
Mushrooms giggle, fairies prance,
In the dark, there's quite the dance.

Snakes in scarves, so sly and slick,
Tell tall tales, they're quite the trick.
With a slither and a spin,
They draw the smiles, invite us in.

Deep within the lively wood,
Creatures chuckle, all feels good.
Leaves rustle, chiming with jest,
In this abyss, we feel so blessed.

Winks exchanged from tree to tree,
Joyful whispers, come and see!
In this green, where laughter grows,
Chortles flow as friendship shows.

Joyful Knots

In the grove where giggles twine,
Watch the branches twist and dine.
Squirrels dance with hats of cheese,
Tickling trunks, swaying with ease.

Breezes hum a silly tune,
Bouncing high like a bright balloon.
Laughter echoes, soft and sweet,
As tiny critters tap their feet.

Nature's jesters play their part,
With a wink and a sprightly start.
Frogs in bow ties croak with flair,
While shadows whirl through sunny air.

Oh, the antics that unfold,
In leafy realms where fun is gold.
Join the frolic, come along,
In this jestful, joyous song.

The Cheerful Chiaroscuro

In the dappled light, shadows prance,
Every rustle sparks a chance.
Sunbeams play hide and seek,
While giggling flowers start to peak.

Bright bumblebees in a race,
Buzzing round with a silly grace.
Wobbling worms in a tiny march,
Splitting sides, like a lively arch.

Dancing leaves in a gentle breeze,
Flutter down like joyful tease.
Whispers stir, secrets unfold,
As the woods break into gold.

With each chuckle, spirits rise,
Nature's jokes, a sweet surprise.
In this light, mischief thrives,
Bringing laughter to our lives.

Grins Among the Leaves

In the branches, smiles bloom wide,
Bouncing bugs with silly pride.
Crickets chirp a merry beat,
As the forest finds its seat.

Mice wear masks of leafy green,
Flaunting roles in nature's scene.
With every rustle, jokes collide,
As the ferns whisper, side by side.

What a sight, these woodland jesters,
Hosting laughter, quirky testers.
Winks of sun through thick-set trees,
Summoning giggles carried by the breeze.

In each nook, a chuckle hides,
Amidst the roots where humor bides.
Join the throng, let laughter soar,
In the glen, forevermore.

Revelry in the Roots

Underneath where shadows play,
The merry gnomes keep gloom at bay.
Sprouting jokes from the rich, dark earth,
Each chuckle dances, full of mirth.

Beneath the bark, a party swells,
With tales of old that each one tells.
Mushrooms giggle, soft and spry,
As beetles twirl in a swirling sky.

Roots entwined in elaborate knots,
Holding secrets, silly thoughts.
With every rustle, we can hear,
Nature's jest, clear and near.

In the twirling, spinning ground,
Laughter blooms, hilarity found.
Join the roots, forever, too,
Where fun and joy will see you through.

Mirth Amongst the Moss

Beneath the shade of leafy cheer,
Frogs croak jokes that all can hear.
Squirrels dance with acorn hats,
As giggles bounce from furry spats.

The sun peeks through, with golden rays,
A jolly breeze joins in the plays.
Mossy mats where all can rest,
Nature's charm, we're truly blessed.

The playful breeze stirs up a sound,
Laughter bubbles from the ground.
Each mischievous twist and sneer,
Brings smiles to every creature here.

So join the fun, let worries fly,
With every chuckle, spirits high.
In mossy realms where giggles bloom,
We find our joy, dispel the gloom.

The Tickled Trunk

A trunk so wide, it's full of glee,
Whispers secrets from a tree.
As butterflies dance on a whim,
Even shadows seem to grin.

The woodpecker plays a lively beat,
While critters gather, oh so sweet.
Branches sway, in jolly jest,
Nature's humor is the best.

A fox strides in with a clever prance,
Joining in the woodland dance.
With every rustle, games arise,
In this realm of twinkling eyes.

So when you hear that joyful crack,
It's laughter echoing, no lack.
In woods where the happy spirits roam,
We'll find our hearts call this place home.

Whimsical Woodlands

In whimsical woods where giggles play,
Trees wear smiles throughout the day.
Rabbits hop in funny flair,
Every leaf sings, joy is rare.

With every rustle, a story's born,
Of playful spirits, bright and worn.
Even the brook's bubbly song,
Invites us to join where we all belong.

Crickets chirp a joking tune,
Amidst the glow of a silver moon.
The merry winds twist and twirl,
Bringing laughter around the world.

So lose yourself in this enchanted space,
Where every creature wears a face.
With whimsy weaving through the air,
In these woods, there's nothing to spare.

Jolly Echoes of Nature

Echoes ripple through the trees,
Carrying laughter on a breeze.
A chattering chipmunk, quick and sly,
Makes the flowers laugh and sigh.

Gliding clouds wear giggling grins,
As the sun plays peek-a-boo, spins.
The forest floor, a stage so grand,
Where tickles spring from nature's hand.

The whispers of the breeze confound,
Tickling toes upon the ground.
From branch to branch, the joyous call,
Makes us smile, makes us all.

So listen close, enjoy the sound,
In jolly echoes, joy is found.
In every nook, a chuckle stays,
In this realm where laughter plays.

Radiant Roots of Laughter

In a garden where giggles grow,
Ticklish petals sway to and fro.
A breeze whispers jokes, full of cheer,
And the trees chuckle loud, oh so clear.

Beneath the sun, the flowers dance,
Each bloom is caught in a merry trance.
With roots that wiggle and twist around,
They spread joy deep in the ground.

The daisies don hats, a sight to behold,
While the tulips share stories, quite bold.
With each silly tale, the laughter spreads,
As the garden's heart fills with fun, it treads.

So come take a stroll, let your cares all drift,
Among the blossoms, where laughter's a gift.
In this playful patch, joy knows no bounds,
Where the spirit of fun in each petal resounds.

Frolicsome Flora

In a meadow bright, the flowers conspire,
To tickle the skies and lift spirits higher.
With petals that giggle in the warm, soft light,
They cast out their charms, a whimsical sight.

With bees in the air buzzing tunes oh so sweet,
The flora will dance, oh what a treat!
A daffodil winks, and the sunflowers grin,
As each little creature joins in with a spin.

The daisies make capers, the violets tease,
In this frolicsome glade, all worries do cease.
From the roots to the buds, the laughter does climb,
In the heart of the flora, it's always prime time.

So come take a moment, relax and enjoy,
The jests of the blossoms, like any good ploy.
In this vibrant place where humor takes flight,
Every petal and leaf glistens with delight.

The Mirthful Wilderness

In the woods where the shadows play tricks,
The trees snicker softly, their laughter in flicks.
Branches entwined whisper secrets so sly,
While the critters below let out giggles that fly.

The forest is filled with a jovial air,
With mushrooms in hats, all tall and quite rare.
The squirrels are jesters, they leap and they bound,
As the echoes of laughter bounce all around.

With bushes that chuckle at silly old tales,
And rivers that gurgle with whimsical wails,
Each nook tells a story, unique and profound,
In this mirthful place, pure joy can be found.

So wander the paths where hilarity brews,
Where every green corner might just sing the blues.
In the heart of the wild, humor reigns true,
Let the laughter of nature invite you anew.

Laughter from Above

Look up in the sky, it's a funny old sight,
Clouds wearing faces, all airy and light.
With their giggles and chuckles that drift from afar,
They sprinkle the world with joy like a star.

The sun beams down with a mischievous wink,
As shadows below dance and spin in sync.
A rainbow whispers jokes to the breeze,
Bringing chuckles and cheer with such effortless ease.

The moon at night shares tales of delight,
Casting laughter softly in the stillness of night.
Each twinkling star joins the raucous refrain,
Creating a symphony of giggles that reign.

So gaze to the heavens, let humor take flight,
As laughter from above fills your heart with light.
In this boundless expanse, let your spirit roam free,
For the joys of the sky are a treat for all to see.

Twinkling Eyes of the Trunk

In the woods, a trunk so grand,
Wears a grin, a quirky brand.
With twinkling eyes, it winks and says,
"Join the dance! Let's laugh all day!"

Branches sway, a playful cheer,
Tickling leaves, drawing near.
Squirrel spins in a joyful loop,
As birds giggle, sharing the scoop.

Mossy carpet, a cozy bed,
Where shadows hide, and giggles spread.
The whispers of the breeze ignite,
A symphony of pure delight.

Old bark cracks with tales so bright,
Of woodland pranks, a silly sight.
Underneath, the critters play,
In nature's game, they laugh away.

Fables of the Frolicsome Timber

In a grove where stories sprout,
Timber talks, without a doubt.
Each knot a clue, each curve a jest,
Fables told from roots to crest.

Woodpeckers drum a jolly beat,
As shadows twirl on nimble feet.
With every tap, the bark joins in,
Whirlpool of laughter, a perfect spin.

Mushrooms giggle, all in a row,
In a cap-and-gown, they steal the show.
Nature's jesters, bold and spry,
While fireflies wink as they float by.

The tapestry of rustling trees,
Hums with joy, fills the breeze.
Echoes bounce from trunk to trunk,
Telling tales with sass and funk.

Jubilant Breeze Through the Canopy

A breeze sails through the leafy dome,
Whispering secrets, calling home.
It twirls the branches, swings the vines,
Sparking giggles amid the pines.

Fluttering leaves join in the game,
Chasing shadows, never the same.
With each rustle, a hearty shriek,
Under the canopy, joyfully sleek.

Sunlight dances on the ground,
Tickling toes, wisdom profound.
Nature chuckles, a raucous shout,
Inviting all, come laugh it out.

A parade of critters leaps high,
Wings and paws in a merry tie.
Together they weave a spell so fun,
As the jubilant breeze claims everyone.

Smile of the Silent Sentinel

In the heart of the woods, a guardian stands,
With a sage-like smile and weathered hands.
He listens close to the whispers near,
And chuckles softly at tales we hold dear.

His bark, a tapestry of decades gone,
Knots that show where the laughs have drawn.
Each ring a memory, each scar a jest,
A silent sentinel of nature's fest.

Creeping vines share stories too,
Of acorn antics and hopscotch dew.
When rabbits giggle, and frogs all croak,
The gentle giant just beams and stokes.

Embraced by the night, the stars all gleam,
Underneath the moon's silvery beam.
In this haven of chuckles, where spirits blend,
The silent sentinel welcomes each friend.

Peppered with Joy

In the garden where giggles bloom,
Dancing leaves shake off the gloom.
A ticklish breeze whispers delight,
As shadows play in morning light.

Riddles rustle among the trees,
Swaying branches, a jolly tease.
Laughter spills like drops of rain,
Filling hearts with sweet refrain.

Merriment in the Mossy Patch

Beneath the canopy of green,
Jokes are shared, a playful scene.
Fungi giggle, and mushrooms sway,
In this mossy hideaway.

A squirrel jests, a fox joins in,
With every twist, the fun begins.
Stones chuckle with a gentle bounce,
As laughter echoes all around.

The Happy Hollow

In a hollow where chuckles dwell,
A jolly tune begins to swell.
A bunny hops with gleeful cheer,
As wonder fills the atmosphere.

Sunbeams dance on playful streams,
Filling the world with silly dreams.
Each echo brings a grin anew,
In this playful space for two.

Trees with a Smile

Tall trunks rise, a friendly gaze,
With branches swaying in a craze.
Each leaf a giggle, soft and light,
They wink at clouds drifting in sight.

A rustling cheer is in the air,
As critters pause to share a flair.
Nature's joy, a wondrous style,
Every corner filled with a smile.

Mirthful Shadows at Dusk

In the twilight's gentle kiss,
Shadows dance with playful bliss.
Whispers echo, giggles sound,
Joy is woven all around.

Squirrels chuckle, birds take flight,
Branches bend with pure delight.
Rustling leaves, a merry cheer,
Nature's laughter drawing near.

Beneath the moon's soft gleaming light,
Every creature, spirits bright.
Twisted tales that trees recite,
Fill the air with pure delight.

In this realm where jokers sing,
A tapestry of joy they bring.
As day yields to the night so sweet,
Laughter fills each heart and beat.

Jests Amongst the Leaves

Amidst the branches, jests take flight,
Leaves a-chuckle, oh what a sight!
Breezes tease with tickling sounds,
In this realm, pure joy abounds.

Frolicsome critters in a race,
Wager their wins in a merry chase.
Swaying grasses join the fun,
Every leaf a trickster spun.

In every nook, a smile gleams,
Life's absurdity woven in dreams.
Echoes of joy fill the air,
A symphony beyond compare.

As dusk arrives, the laughter grows,
Mirth unfurling, the world it knows.
In leaves and logs, with glee align,
Nature's humor, forever divine.

Sylvan Serenade of Joy

Under the canopy, a giggle rings,
Nature's choir, the laughter sings.
Every rustle, every croak,
Bursting forth with joyful joke.

Sunlight dapples, laughter sways,
In the woods, the fun displays.
Robins chuckle at the play,
While squirrels leap in grand ballet.

Bumbling beetles, silly prance,
In this world, all take a chance.
With every snicker, every cheer,
A tapestry of joy draws near.

Beneath the stars, the stories flare,
Of playful times and joy to share.
So join the dance, come lend an ear,
In this glen where all find cheer.

Laughter in the Heart of the Forest

Deep in the woods, where whispers play,
Laughter blooms in a bright bouquet.
Blossoms giggle, branches sway,
Every corner holds a joke in stay.

Trees wear grins, and shadows tease,
A hidden world of playful ease.
With every rustle, cheer takes flight,
A symphony of pure delight.

Chipmunks chuckle in their race,
While turtles laugh at their own pace.
Dancing ants to rhythms loud,
Creating joy, making us proud.

As night descends and stars ignite,
The forest glows with laughter bright.
Join the chorus, let spirits soar,
In this green haven, forevermore.

Nature's Heartbeat of Laughter

In the woods where critters play,
Silly sounds brighten the day.
Squirrels joke with the trees,
While the breeze joins with ease.

Frogs croak in a quirky tune,
Dancing 'neath the smiling moon.
Leaves rustle, full of glee,
Nature's giggles wild and free.

Watch the rabbit's funny hops,
Over mushrooms, and then plops.
A chorus of chuckling birds,
Sending joy in cheerful words.

With every rustle, every peep,
The forest wakes from slumber deep.
Echoes bounce through branches spry,
As laughter lights the azure sky.

Hidden Groves and Grinning Faces

In secret glades where fairies dwell,
Giggles rise from each small knell.
Mushrooms smile with painted flair,
Whispers dance upon the air.

Raccoons in masks, a playful sight,
Stealing snacks beneath the night.
Trees lean close, adorned in wit,
With leafy laughs, we all commit.

Dancing shadows, prancing sprites,
Swirling joy in moonlit nights.
Nature's jesters, soft and low,
Share their secrets as they glow.

In every nook, a joke unfolds,
The forest tells its tales of old.
With every chuckle, hearts embrace,
Hidden groves and grinning face.

Chuckles from the Depths of the Woods

Deep within the sagebrush high,
Funny tales where echoes lie.
Bushy tails and nibbled leaves,
Nature's laughter never leaves.

Beetles march in silly rows,
Tickling toes of sleepy crows.
The owls wink with playful might,
Under stars that twinkle bright.

Whispers flutter near the stream,
As the fish join in the dream.
With every splash, a giggle flows,
In this realm where humor grows.

Mossy patches hold delights,
As shadows play, igniting nights.
In this space where joy resides,
Chuckles dance on gentle tides.

Harmony in the Whimsical Wilderness

Amidst the trees, a band does play,
With frogs on drums and birds in sway.
Laughter spirals through the air,
Joyful moments everywhere.

With each rustle, tales unfold,
The woods alive with stories told.
Sunlight glimmers, skipping glee,
Nature's song, bright jubilee.

Caterpillars wear tiny hats,
While crickets dance with little spats.
The brook hums a quirky tune,
In the glow of the smiling moon.

This wilderness with whimsy's grace,
Holds a treasure in each embrace.
In harmony, our spirits rise,
Laughter painted in the skies.

Cheerful Vines and Wind-Kissed Dreams

Vines twirl and dance with glee,
Whimsical friends in jubilee.
They tickle the breeze with playful cheer,
Spreading laughter far and near.

Sunlight spills like liquid gold,
Stories of mirth yet to be told.
Beneath the canopy, giggles bloom,
Spinning joy, dispelling gloom.

Leaves flutter, whispering tunes,
Bouncing laughter 'neath the moons.
Crisp air carries their merry sounds,
As happiness twirls and bounds.

In this haven, fun takes flight,
Chasing shadows, morning light.
With every step, a chuckle flows,
In this land where joy just grows.

Whispers of Joy in the Gnarled Trees

Gnarled branches twist and sway,
Mischievous sparks in playful play.
Leaves burst forth with sneaky grins,
As laughter in the canopy spins.

Bouncing shadows dance on ground,
Joyful echoes all around.
Rustling leaves, a jovial cheer,
Each branch bent low to lend an ear.

Squirrels scamper with delight,
Chasing breezes, pure and bright.
Nature's creatures join the fun,
Under the gaze of a bright sun.

In the hush, a giggle hides,
As whimsy walks with leafy strides.
In these woods, the spirit beams,
Bringing forth the sweetest dreams.

Whispers of the Woods

Through shadows deep where secrets dwell,
A friendly titter starts to swell.
In every nook, a chuckle rests,
As nature hosts her silly jest.

Sprightly blooms in colors bright,
Bend and sway, a merry sight.
In the air, a soft refrain,
Whispered laughs, like gentle rain.

Mossy carpets hold the glee,
Beneath the boughs, wild and free.
The sun peeks through, all aglow,
To join the fun beneath the bow.

With every step, the forest grins,
A chorus sings, the magic spins.
Joy unfolds in each small scene,
In the heart of glades serene.

Echoes of a Jolly Tree

A tree stands tall, full of cheer,
With whispers echoing far and near.
Its branches sway with stories bright,
Welcoming all to join the flight.

Beneath its shade, laughter flows,
Where secrets hide in greens and throes.
Swaying leaves spark playful dreams,
In the sun, the joy just beams.

The wind hums sweet, a merry tune,
Singing of fun beneath the moon.
Every ripple, every breeze,
Brings merriment among the trees.

So come and play in its embrace,
Join in the dance, a frolicsome chase.
A jubilant spirit fills the air,
In this land of laughter and flair.

www.ingramcontent.com/pod-product-compliance
Lightning Source LLC
Chambersburg PA
CBHW051653160426
43209CB00004B/885